a man
who doesn't have
the strength
to love you

should not be allowed
the power to break you

you go searching
for a love
that has always lived
beneath your skin
between your bones
inside your heart

his inability to remain faithful
is a confession of his weakness

avoid weak men

any man who chooses you
over the one they're with
will choose someone
while with you

some of you aren't looking for a summer fling. some of you are learning to be alone, especially if it means living without drama. some of you are happily single because being alone is better than being used.

will there ever come a time
where your heart won't miss
the person who broke it

i wish you knew
just how happy you could be
on your own, without him

but heartbreak takes time
to transform into a lesson

somewhere along the way
you suffered for so long
that you decided that heartache
was a symptom of love

not knowing that if he truly loved you
there would be no reason for you
to pick up this book
and if he truly cared
these words would not have meant
so much to you as your eyes
scan this page in hopes of healing

somewhere along the way
you lost yourself
and i'm just hoping
that you eventually
rediscover who you've always been

someone worth loving

love me when i'm weary
and teary-eyed
from being let down
by the world

love me as if i was perfect
even with my flaws
clearly visible for all to see

love me through the brokenness
that lives within my heart
love me regardless of the pain
that i struggle to survive

love me with a truth
that drowns all lies
love me with a peace
that destroys the chaos
living in my soul

just love me

fuck you
for pretending to be
the type of person
she could love

fuck you
for bull shitting her
while making promises
you were too weak to keep

fuck you
because it's your fault
that she's reading this now
searching for words
that'll soothe her soul

fuck you
for all the ways
you fucked up her life
fuck you
for forcing her
down a path of misery
and disappointment

Insecure men cheat. It was never you, it was never your fault. You loved a man who hates himself. You loved a man who is too weak to love you in the way you deserve.

so much fuckin yet everyone is so empty and lonely.

he doesn't miss you. he's just bored with the woman he left you for, and so he'll return if you allow it. don't allow it.

men always want a second chance, but if you were to treat him the way he treats you, he'd leave.

you are more than enough, and he will never be worth it.

I hope you find a heart that will love you through your brokenness.

you were poetry
before words existed

woman
never compromise your strength
to make a weak man appear strong

You are something unusual and every day, you happen to yourself.

You can't find peace with a man who is comfortable with destroying your heart.

the women with the most painful stories have the most profound love to give.

It's scary how the worst guys are the best at making you believe that they deserve all the love that lives within your heart.

he took so much out of you
but you remained whole

you are unusually profound and rare
do not settle for a love that feels mediocre

Do not look for love in a man who treats you like he hates you.

He hesitated when you asked him to choose you.
don't hesitate to leave.

Phone full of contacts and still lonely as fuck.

So many good women sacrifice their dreams to be a part of nightmares created by lovers who will never love them.

Love without compromising the peace in your heart.

Some people can't find the words to describe their pain, and so they claim to be okay while breaking from within.

all those bodies

and still nobody

you're still lonely

she was still winter
during summer nights

she is a vigorous raging flame that can't be put out.

Stop falling in love with weak men with empty promises and no potential.

Stop giving your heart to someone who only ever wants your body.

The first ones to teach you about love are the people incapable of truly loving you.

you are magic

even at your most broken

loving someone is never an excuse to allow them to treat
your heart like shit.

Imagine someone loving you just as much as you've loved the wrong people.

Stop searching for healing in the same relationship that hurts your soul.

She's strong enough to be gentle and brave enough to love without conditions. Don't take that for granted.

She broke her own rules to love you but never again.

It's never too late to say " nah, I'm good " to those who take your presence for granted.

I hope you find someone who understands how to love you at your most broken.

You have suffered enough. It's time to thrive.

tonight, she's just trying to forget someone who was never worth the love she gave.

feeling broken
doesn't mean
unlovable

the problem is
her heart is still falling
for someone
too weak
to ever catch her

may your nights
be filled with the courage
to keep letting go of people
who no longer deserve you

midnight came, and she was no longer afraid of losing you.

you deserve better, and if you meant something to him, then you wouldn't have related to this.

the wildest storm
is a woman's love

heartache does not
deserve you

you are the wild
that could stand firm
beneath storms and not be moved

it hurts to be overlooked and neglected, and you just want to make sense to someone.

he's just a bad plot twist. a man who claims to love you but disappoints you in the end.

you just want someone with eyes that are only
committed to seeing you.

the issue with being kind is that you often find yourself giving a fuck about people who were never worth your energy.

SAY THIS OUTLOUD

I'm not sorry for wanting more than you were willing to give. I won't apologize for knowing that I deserved more.

The way he apologizes with no intention of changing his behavior is abuse.

You found yourself loving the wrong person, you lost yourself in return. The many days and nights you spent blaming yourself without realizing that you were never the issue. No, you were never in the wrong. Your love is a language that weak people will never be able to comprehend and this is why those relationships never last. You can't keep a person who isn't meant to be in your life. Even if you still have them in your heart.

I wanted to speak directly to you because you've been blaming yourself for the brokenness that exists within your relationship. You've been so hard on yourself because you're made to think that you're not good enough but you've done all you can and no amount of effort will save a relationship that is no longer worthy of your energy and love.

I know it's difficult to believe in yourself when the person you've given everything to takes it all for granted. I know it's hard to love yourself through the heartache you feel, and it's hard to be gentle with yourself when you're too busy caring for someone who never makes an effort for you but inside you lives the will to survive and the strength to move on and I hope this message reaches you in your time of need.

Sincerely, r.h. Sin

Some people will fail you, even when you've given them your all. It's easy to blame yourself when in all honesty, the truth is...not everyone has the heart you have, and it's okay to walk away from those who do not appreciate the energy you give them.

Here you are, feeling weak because you've found it difficult to walk away from them. Even after they break your heart, even after they've continuously let you down. I think you're too hard on yourself. You're too critical of yourself while ignoring the fact that the real problem is not you. Your ability to love someone is not a weakness, and your struggle to move on is just a sign of how much you genuinely care about this person. I want you to know that love can often feel one-sided, especially when you're with the wrong person but being with the wrong person is not a fate in which you have to accept, and you are not obligated to stay where you're unhappy. I know these words may not mean that much because let's be honest, I'm just a stranger who wants nothing but the best for you, but I do hope you read this and take these words to heart. Your story isn't over, and as soon as you walk away, the sooner you can begin a new chapter, a better chapter. I hope these words reach the person who needs this the most.

Take care, r.h. Sin

You're here, you're reading this now, and I'd like to first start by thanking you. Your strength is a source of inspiration, and your will to survive has inspired me in this very moment.

You're going through a rough patch, and it's been a tough year. You entered this year filled with love and optimism, and at this point, you're nearly running on empty. Your heart and mind tired from caring for the wrong person and thinking about someone who isn't worth your thoughts. You have suffered for far too long, and I'll be honest with you. There is still a bit of heartache left to go, but the pain will make you stronger.

I admire you and your ability to break down all walls and obstacles that stand in your way of happiness. I praise you because even though it's hard, you're reading this now while surviving yet another war. I'll be here for you, and I'll try to encourage you as much as I can, but you mustn't give up on yourself. You have what it takes to be your own hero as you've proven time and time again that you are more than enough and fully capable. You're going to be okay, and it'll get better.

Sincerely, r.h. Sin

There is something divine about her existence. The way she roams the earth like wind, an image provoking the idea of an angel figuring out that she can fly. The allure of her presence, driving me wild, keeping me inspired while falling into a well of bliss. She's magic.

Several poems are living within you. Some of which have never been read or spoken out loud. They're like melodic stories of heartache and survival. You only tell them to yourself and perhaps the moon during the midnight hour. You lose so much sleep at that particular time. Playing out scenarios of moments you wish went differently, struggling with yourself as you fight for your life, love, and your sanity. You have several poems residing deep within you, giving more meaning to the chaos that plagues your heart and the triumphs of your breakthroughs. Your fear of being betrayed or judged has kept your heart sealed. Afraid of being taken for granted or misunderstood, you keep it all to yourself. You have several poems embedded into your existence, and when you're ready to share them all, I hope that person appreciates your story.

Some of you have struggled with this idea of getting to that point in which you no longer give a fuck as much as you used to. Some of you have been struggling with the task of letting go of a relationship that is no longer worthy of your energy. What a place to be, the moment where you start focusing on yourself and your new journey, rather than feeling stuck in a relationship with someone who will never deserve your energy, time, and love. If you're reading this now, if you're currently struggling with letting go….I hope you know that you are fully capable. I hope you realize that you must love yourself through the pain and confusion. You must continue to choose yourself, and you must continue to find ways to find the courage to walk away. You have already proven that you are strong enough to love someone unconditionally, and this is how I know that you are also strong enough to move forward with your life. I feel like I'm reaching the person who needs to be reached. I feel like you're reading this now. I feel like you're tired, you're weary from the fight, but I also know that you will find the victory you've been searching for. Please don't give up on yourself. I promise not to give up on you. Hopefully, these words help.

I don't know you, but I think you're lying there in a dark room with little light, this book in your hand. Losing sleep because you're thinking about the one person you wish you could walk away from. I don't know you, but I wish you well. I wish you'd find the courage to move on. I hope you read these words and be reminded that you are capable of setting yourself free. I hope you read this and realize that you are not alone. You might even find that many people feel exactly how you feel at this very moment. I don't know you, and yet, I hope you find yourself. I hope you find a love that allows your heart to rest. Take care.

I hope you enjoyed the content here and I hope you find more of my words whenever you need them the most. My name is r.h. Sin and I'd like to take this moment to say thank you for giving me a portion of your mind, your heart and time.